Gone to Marzipan

Also by Ralph Hawkins:

English Literature
Well, You Could Do
The Word from the One
Soft in the Brains
Tell Me No More And Tell Me
Birds, Cattle, Fish & Flies
At Last Away
Within & Without
Writ
Routes & Abrasions
Flecks
Pelt
Part One Puškin
The Coiling Dragon / The Scarlet Bird / The White Tiger /
    A Blue & Misted Shroud
Pool
The Primeval Atom
The MOON, The Chief Hairdresser (highlights)
Quaoar (with Kelvin Corcoran and Alan Halsey)

(with Bob Cobbing)
G Curled Ribbon
a split
A Quonk
Signatures or the Wasp Under Custard
Gloria
The Next Morning
Everyday Pursuits

Gone to Marzipan

R ALPH H AWKINS

Shearsman Books
Exeter

First published in the United Kingdom in 2009 by
Shearsman Books Ltd
58 Velwell Road
Exeter EX4 4LD

www.shearsman.com

ISBN 978-1-84861-021-7

Copyright © Ralph Hawkins, 2009.

The right of Ralph Hawkins to be identified as the author of this work has been asserted by him in accordance with the Copyrights, Designs and Patents Act of 1988. All rights reserved.

Acknowledgements
Some of these poems have previously been published in
Angel Exhaust, Poetry Review, Skald, Shearsman,
The Gig and *The North*.

Contents

Poetics	9
she left a note	10
they had lovely hair in the cinema of the 50's and 60's	11
today's fish swim deeper in dark pressure	12
it's free Tibet day	13
Bewarewolf Poem	14
The Alphabet (A Cognitive Map of Civilization)	16
Wolves (a diptych, two sides of the same coin))	18
Photographs	19
I take pictures	20
the keyboard has a voice	21
this is here – soft wet snow against glass	22
she wrote animals and lived with them	23
Iceberg	25
The Hudson River School Motif	26
Maxter Gold	27
Porkies	28
The Quiet American	29
Saturday Morning Pictures	30
Gaslight	31
Pull My Daisy	32
Dr Zhivago	33
The Searcher	34
The life of Georges Simenon (Extracts)	35
In The Ruins	37
The Man who Fought With Rats	38
The Insane One (Men of Power)	39
Corned Beef	40
Rem Koolhaas	41
it will not run out for millions of	42
nightingales at the feeder	43
list the members of a family sheltered by one roof	44
115 million copies of the Ikea catalogue printed world wide	45
Human Development	46
Descriptions of Huts (Orders of Survival)	47

blows of wind and rain buffeted them	48
there are huts in the North of Europe	49
apparently swallows, rooks, bees and storks	50
shelter from severities with reed and cane	51
In Monomotapa all the dwellings are of wood	52
the name of the inventor of perfume is not known	53
Shepherds	54
Some Questions Concerning Civilization	55
the road festooned	56
the waterfront is lined with mansions	57
The View From Space (Sub-Orbital)	58
Themes For Developing A Treaty	59
The Age of Warring	60
Dirk Brocade	61
Heidegger	62
Chaise Longue	64
The Greenhouse Effect	66
Che Guevara's Cigar	68
Casino	69
The Good Shepherd	70
Anthropology	74
Natural Material	75
The Making of Mong	76
The Citadel of Love	77
Moon Rush (for Yuri Gargarin)	78
A Bright New Thing Has Dawned	80
Three Hudson River School Poems	81
Viagra From Goat Island	82
Coincidence	83
Frans Van Meris: The Soldier And The Prostitute	84
Mount Ida Zeus	85
African Inquisition	86
Sierra Leone	87
Contradictions	88
L'homme du train	89
Transport	90

The Queen of Puddings

she will not	93
the sentence	94
I look	95
Leading	96
Nineteen	97
Consumer Choice	98
we should never	99
what a day	100
what now	101
I wondered	102
more	103
gulf	104
white rush	105
the queen of puddings	106
melts	107
sky-diver	108
nip and tuck	109
shades	110
health care	111
tantalize	112
dance lessons	113
volvic	114
plain facts	115
something to look forward to	116
wishful thinking	117
future plans	118
my blood ran	119

Poetics

1. We understand the factors governing present day poetic distribution
2. These affinities have not changed through time
3. Present and past distributions are and were not in equilibrium
4. Modern analogues pre-exist
5. The taphonomy of a poetic assemblage can be established
6. This assemblage is biased by contamination of source material
7. Poems can be identified to a meaningful level of taxonomic resolution

the wind blah blahs
up to 20,000 generations of beetles
munching on wood

dark pollen rains into pools
ambered scent fills the air
glistens at your neck

she left a note

Gone to Marzipan

I looked it up in a dictionary

The fallen nuts make a dog paste in the sand

They list the ingredients in the hotel

The young girl in 127

It produces millions of dollars

At Christmas they charge treble for a double

Did she mean Mozambique

Resin wafting from pine

The almond of her thighs

they had lovely hair in the cinema of the 50's and 60's

technicolor cinemascope

but was it real

Catherine Deneuve had a headscarf★

Victor Mature a pout

you also had lovely hair

I wrote *I Love Lucy* for Andrew

Donald Duck as Natty Bumppo

★well after *Belle de Jour*

there was Biblical rain

when only true lovers kissed

today's fish swim deeper in dark pressure

death by lethal injection

another city bursts into flame urb by urb by urb

sweeping the globe in cycles

this we know from the Venusians (based in Virginia in 1606)

held dreams of world domination*

prone to smallpox, malnutrition

swamp fever

at war with Spain or

*terra incognito

it's free Tibet day

the air shimmers and the trappings of state produce varied menus

there are many offers at hand in trading relations

oil leaving gaps in consciousness

there are still good deals to be had

in changing body-count rules

there is happiness in recycling old dogmas

the myth of perfectibility

today I read

I will meet the man of my dreams

provider of breakfast cuddles

the Dalai Lama worries about his last breath

that it may *not* be his last breath

Bewarewolf Poem

> *you know I'm the wolf baby*
> *you know I stays in the wood*
> *well when you get in trouble*
> *you call the wolf out of the wood*
>   *Howlin' Wolf*

Olf Larson stepped out of his Finnish dacha
or was it a Volvo
pine trees in blue

running in front of him an encircling figuration of paw prints
leading off into
Cat People like moments

Man With Dog 1953 by Francis Bacon

Joe Stalin in his dacha

Absolut Vodka

Olf changing his name to Gunter
changing his erstwhile car to a Golf Automatic

wolves out to get you
switching from one thing to another
trading piss mark signs as stigmata

what is there for a male wolf—career, mortgage, she-wolves—
        wolf cubs
St. Stephen Suckled by a Doe
St. Nicholas of Tolentino Calms a Storm
St. Francis and The Wolf of Gubbio

Gunter worked out at a Health Spa
ice-cold skies
splendid mountain views
a cold star with a *sickle* moon
the Siberian wastes full of timber, oil and gold
enough to make a killing

money ascribed with blood
Sassetta's *Madonna of the Snow*
the halo of St. Francis embossed **PATRICIA PAUPERUM**
Olf's cousin the Siberian Tiger
stocking the freezer with shark steak and swordfish
alpine plants in superstores
on the urbs outskirts and byways of leisure
passed *Swimmies* the Vietnamese Fighting Fish
what the English call hobbies
Gunter discovers *Pet World* is a brothel

THE ALPHABET
(A COGNITIVE MAP OF CIVILIZATION)

King Ape followed by King Bee
(or is that Queen B?)
What of Aristotle (a different line)
follow the bouncing ball
King Crab Stick
That's Ari Aristotle the ship magnate
(Where did the Minoans come from?)
the descent into poetic Anarchy

Should I take up gardening instead
The ABC of Gardening
a trellis

solitude

Gramsci's *Prison Notebooks*

and happiness, what is that

Bush Fire
Texas expansion
To wear cowboy boots

The gun lobby
Even the actor who played Moses in Moses and Monotheism
realizes the quest for oil

The Black Dahlia
The Petrified Forest

The Blast Shelter
(shadows of the dead)

ah Leslie Howard

are we now on W

King Wang?

Waylon Jennings or Hank Wangford

Don't I dare

WOLVES (A DIPTYCH, TWO SIDES OF THE SAME COIN)

Recently I've been thinking
Of making a late marriage to the daughter
Of a wolf butcher
We'd escape from it all to an island under an endless star-lit sky
There'd be a big welcome kiss on the harbourmaster's wall
You'd have kiss-curled hair (early Doris Day) and rose lipstick
You'd wear a snow-white dress sequinned with star-gems
I'd hold the diskette of the world sun-bolt bright in my hand
We'd begin a circus
I'd become a wolf tamer
Finally abandoning my fascination with market economies

I'd marry the harbourmaster under perfectly normal conditions
I'd be the profligate blonde
There'd be a big wet kiss on his lips
He'd have kiss-curled hair (Rick Nelson)
I'd wear my white dress encrusted with star-gems
We'd go to Nacogdoches
I'd hold the reins of the world in my hand
(or was it Kansas?)
I'd embrace the market economy
I'd run off with the Mexican circus owner
I'd marry a Medicine Man
and feed our children to the wolves

Photographs

one city amongst many of rubble
Soviet soldiers outside the Brandenburg Gate
a dead horse flayed for flesh
France 1896, animals appear in Auguste Lumière's
Le Déjeuner du chat
Auguste Charpentier's *Rat d'égout*
even animals from the city zoo
they are part of everyday life
a duck or two
one shaking itself in flight
only yesterday

I take pictures
odd things, the Madonna, the children
the shutter clicks
the sheets hanging out in a strong wind (Tiree)
a toy windmill turns (wind farm) off
screen in the poem
reading from their emptied pockets
charm bracelet, stones
echoing on the contact sheet
only imagination printing memory on the written word

the keyboard has a voice
sonal and intimate, picture torn, cut
other devices—sudden changes of place and time
arranging from the private and personal
the contingent instability of meaning
the here and not here of your likeness
it's like a pencil
I can write things I never say

this is here—soft wet snow against glass
deictic from the Greek for show
there is some fictional and documentary material
improvisation and conscious planning
cohesion maintained across difference
Traudel as a young woman (picture)
he served at Bastion 12 at the Plateau d'Avron near Rosny
(the rat eater Paris Commune)
memory in this instance is a landscape
coloured by thought and feeling
in a motel room in Los Angeles
picture of Nicole and Tom
the tension between two Poles
Traudel was often jealous of Inge
micro-narratives
pictures of instances of the quotidian
crows in January snow
Homer's duck falling lifeless towards a tin bath

she wrote animals and lived with them

in 1959 she published *Tiere mit Familienanschluss*

animals as props are always lovingly close at hand

two little dogs nearby

two are upright while one reclines

one leans forward

another leans backwards into a chair

and a third lies sideways

one wears a hat

two are bareheaded   one reads   one thinks

one poses one smiles one is grave

a third is vacant

two are ready to leave

she had a metempsychotic identification with them

it is contradictory to shoot them

à la goose gun

walking through the forest with her dogs and monkeys

lions and tigers appear

in Regnault's *Hasan et Namoura*

indolently sinking into a cushion

there is a lion carpet

Iceberg

set sail for Boston
via Halifax and Nova Scotia

a chain of milk solids

with Miss May Miss May Knot Miss Maybe Miss You

a bouquet of white

flushed from our excursions

startlingly beautiful

with cherry blossom

melting before our eyes

crumbling and dissolving into the sea

akin to what sometimes we find in sleep

The Hudson River School Motif

the sky ominous above Mount Desert Island 1850

the last of the sun's rays catch a mantle of pink cloud

white chalk to cover red rouge

in the not too far middle distance
casinos, motels and trailer parks

crimson and saffron cluster along the horizon

belts of opal apple-green

a divine from the Swedish Church

the Pentecost

hearing rings of fire *Un Nos Ola Leuad*

a sombre set of associations

the application of words especially to the left of the sky

10,000 leaves like pieces of paper confection

the rocks too speak

no canoes or tepees can be seen

no doggers' paths

no trappers' huts

miniscule birds afloat below the disc of the sun

cloud vapours spill from the brush

Maxter Gold

they arrived in spring and summer when the roads were passable

a polity to be made up of contented home owners

the little ones rode merry-go-rounds
the wooden horse going up and down on
candy striped wooden poles

the rat killer testing his poison
the plastic surgeon
the hospital without medicine
the car bomber

a boy from Kentucky
his girl and their child from Nebraska
when snow was thick on the ground

the developing town was soon run by a handful of bourgeois
       families
lawyers, tradesmen and small shopkeepers

their descendents turning their hands to oil, arms, banking and
       pharmaceuticals

they all wore the same hats and seemingly
kept away from the saloon and dance halls
were women could be hired to tango

under the protection of these controlling influences
one could grow to be confident, hopeful and pragmatic

life as always carrying on much like before

Porkies

I made several false starts in life
pretending to work
in an office
but resisted after five years

office workers peopled my poetry
girls in short skirts
prematurely bald men
bonding after work on Fridays

living several months with a certain Cecil
I thought one day in a small house
I could become an artist
papier collé, photographs, inky words
cloudy tropes

of having a studio
and lots of arty friends

none of whom after Cecil
ever appeared

it was here my fascination
with hidden significance emerged

I laboured hard at my art

looking for the one
who has the face of a thief
the one you can't make out on CCTV

The Quiet American

he flicks through a book
it's a tropical summer and the women are thinly dressed
there are colours, there are always colours in Lee's poems
a car starts, red (backfire) (firecrackers)
I think as he turns the page
there is love scribble on the reverse of an envelope (black)
we will make a journey
I think of Kashmir
Kandahar
children
being removed for surgery

SATURDAY MORNING PICTURES

the words
the syntax
the perceptions involved in reversals
the uncommon order
a thumb is distraught
(the fool's finger)
a submarine won't appear
a straw, a saving one, a reed
up through the swamp water [more later]★
will pierce a word-bubble for air
oblique images connecting memory lines
the Metaphysicals
★arguing over Tarzan
the co-star (I can't recall her name)
beating off a crocodile-
tear, clad only in the ways of animals

Gaslight

I'm putting of the inevitable bout
of manic depression
NOSTALGIA
what you wore I spread on the bed
a tracery of sorts (escapism)
what was large became small
a white one like a lie
a whole field a flower
the night sky just one star
the ice will melt
and the mountain will come into view
I will slip from the face of the earth
out of the country by gaslight
toboggan to safety
FINLANDIA
a toccata, the wind crying all over it
I roll over dreaming of sliding towards Oslo

Pull My Daisy

they said I'd forgotten
I studied reductive thinking
science shaping the future of my thought
for exercise I could put the shot
mail order superseded by buy on line
fast breeder yeast
I'll try anything
my wishes no longer written in invisible ink
now I carry a knife to incise *ansuz*
on my way from Denmark to Norway
to health spa
to roll over in snow
to be birch thrashed
everything appears in visual memory
as its own entity
like a photograph
random observations through coincidence
the point where the background becomes
the foreground as in the work of Robert Frank

Dr Zhivago

who carries the tablet of destinies
birds disappearing across the sky
like falling stars
I read the *timer pings*
she says she has a little left for the weekend
I think of a white city (Moscow)
recalling Dr Zhivago I shiver
what is in the oven
clam chowder
what do Russians eat
I heard beetroot
in one film a sniper hunts a sniper
the other sniper hunts him
in my hand I have a 10 inch long Jing Kung
it could do some damage
it all seems to end in death

Perry Como

Doris Day

Julie Christie?

The Searcher

his constitution was waning
all his thoughts were her
all the ideas he had when young
were now a dry river gulch
smoke signals
were simple signs
she wore a simple enough dress
a lizard whose skin changed
and then the communists came to town
down through the hills and valleys
she left home (abducted by Indians)
married to a jinn who lived in the woods
she said to be handsome he must kiss her
she immaterialised and spoke a lost dialect
she became the wolf who stole his babies
changing the shape of people's thought
I bet she lives in Texas now
and doesn't pay taxes
she is the sort after senorita
he would have cowboy blue eyes
and know Mexican ways

THE LIFE OF GEORGES SIMENON (EXTRACTS)

1. If I could

my eyes follow the soft slope of your throat
five or six times per meal
trying to avoid open heart surgery
If I could swim I'd open an off shore account
in a barge to the Far North
with a ballast of white gold

2. Allergy

it was two hours of the afternoon
when a rash broke out
I covered it with my fur lined coat
scenting my hands with rose
before returning each to a different one
doodling on the window in the first of Spring's rain
all from a gluten allergy

3. The Man of Miserable Appearance

on these autumnal days of low tide
we should not trouble or vex ourselves
it's just a sordid business
having spent the night in infinite rêveuses intensities
surely the goal is to take the sea on board
to pull the collar up
to make better from the cold
to provide for the children
to ward off collapse

4. *Bi-annual Leave*

wake up to more self-medication
in the off-peak hours
tasting giddiness in delirium
all is unreal in this business
in a vague misty landmass
freedom is crime detached from democracy
I take a holiday for my medicine

5. *Counterfeit*

I am about to confess
I have gone under to the Far North
in a barge through the canals of France
where the priest of our lady baptises it
so I can make it to the land of happy
a forgery so I think of the truth this time

In the Ruins

I can taste her words of
too much cayenne and
not enough lipstick (cerise)
I was better in May (pink and white / thorn)
in six months the sheets (white) I cried
dried even though it rained
and tear and pepper gas fill the air
I shall buy binding (love) and duct tape
with which to commit phrasal bonding
I will retain myself on the stair case
five or six times a year

The Man who Fought With Rats

another day at its close draws
a castle of red sand against a low sky
I did not suspect my friends (trust)
the convict with my nougat (sweet one)
more than a mere moment of felicity
the captive man between two women (the polytechnician)
maybe from a high window
a bird catches your hazel eye
a line of snow melts my heart
so much this tackled subject (love)
is of universal interest

THE INSANE ONE (MEN OF POWER)
If they commit crimes then these are not small but great

always the imprint of my step
carries me to the same point
I write to the Prime Minister
a tremulous dialectic
I note the curses in the sky
of blackened puffs and spurts
amongst
a jumble of untruths
lies and reinventions
that's what makes his crimes so interesting
in the end he is willing to kill
a captive of ambition the quasi legend
the one who will only finish when
he holds the bomb between his hands
which from here looks like a familiar landscape
of wrath, of pustules, disease, boils and sores

Corned Beef

a steam of cattle wandering
black through the rain
a semi-coast in the trees and walls
the slow drip drip
movement of the barge through a film
maybe all the way to the Arctic Circle
or anywhere else from 2 to 5 in the morning
dying of lacklustre on a chain-link fence
a fine dust settling on a cold star
a salt-lick at foot
pricks of glitter
he has broken wind and
borrowed money from where the victims live

Rem Koolhaas

the new city is iconographic
the Byzantine Church in Palermo
from the sky the lines weave over
mountains and through summer forests
flushed out into the sea
roads named after Sooty and Sweep

the bulldozer becomes a weapon of destruction

junktime fills junkspace

having a tribal tattoo on the lower back

sipping red tea in the Blossom garden

information teleports across the harbour
gathering shopping points and credits

a red flag sails up the river
to another country for which
there are no available statistics

it will not run out for millions of

the young begin by eating adult faeces until

sipping green tea in the Lotus House

if you look at the map you can see where they prepared to die
their bones found in

reconstructing cities through precision bombing

nightjars singing, yellowhammers
geese gather at the outflows

as a blue flag sails towards Polynesia

furniture made from rattan

they will get in the architects to see which buildings to remove

the great divide

the name of his dog sitting on the White House lawn

now curlews gather in the fields

nightingales at the feeder

looking at the map of migration (Slavs across Europe)
the ship carries scrap metal to China

Doris Day smiles handing the bellboy a fortune cookie
in the p.m. arrange diet problems
a vase of tulip and gentian

the terror of his master's voice

red lines demarcating safe zones

they laugh and smile

eating the faeces of their parents
gnawing on the lives of their enemies

perchance they will never meet face to face

list the members of a family sheltered by one roof
we are holidaying at the Pagoda Inn where
bird painting takes up most of the 3rd wall
lotus flowers are the theme of the day
the roof is partly translucent
Elijah coming to him in a vision
the membrane (peritoneum) providing weather protection
planning to bomb Qatar
and UV reduction
to rubble and death
at this point 665000 civilian deaths
the dark wood where we walk
extracting from natural disorder the order of unmeaning
his dog talking to him in a dream
self supporting pillows acting as thermal insulation
leading the mind into deep deep dark spaces

115 million copies of the Ikea catalogue printed world wide
it is stated in the colophon that
happiness skips one beat of the heart
the allspice bush breaks into flower
from one theme park to another
Thomas Cole contenting himself into his mother's arms
as vivid as the colours in the oil version
leading the mind into ravines
a crescent moon on her thigh
the stars like lilies cluster
picking through the rubble from the bomb
there'd be something to recycle
out of focus pictures across a scattergram of time
like heavy drops of starting rain
was the dog's name Bullet

Human Development

we are still plodding up the lonely
slope towards the summit
of spiritual enlightenment

the city below in the valley
where each man had set forth

a cluster of trees stand out
from the haze of star-like lilies

in the distance the weave of ring roads
flush out into the hinterland
during peak use periods

the luxury residential towers are
prone to cascading systems failure

did precision bombing hit
the wrong building

the hospitals first
leaving the wounded to die

there'd be something to recycle

geese gathering at the outflows

Descriptions of Huts (Orders of Survival)

the building is a wood
as we walk through it
the canopy overwhelms us

a starry laden leafy vault

a half shell (a huge nut case—a case for nuts)

the walker can cut off a limb to stave off cocks and geese

to avoid harm's way

or visit the Hospital of Tropical Medicine
(those big buboes on his heart have still not healed)

it is from Hegel we learn we need water
to set wheels in motion in order to cut wood

swimming (surviving) is the difficult part

out at sea (all at sea) is a drowning dog near a floating log
just passing through the essential carpentry stage

you can just about hear his bark

and here comes the rescue canoe

or is it a coracle

blows of wind and rain buffeted them

the woodland haunts of nymphs

and the whistling song of birds

men barbecuing kebabs   spatchcock chickens

Thai wings

the trees forming a natural chamber

grouped in threes

arranged triangularly

imitating the ancient people of Achaia

we would have a roof over our heads

and tender shoots at our feet

disturbed of late by the sounds of police sirens

the odd echoing yelp of riot, insurrection and social disorder

there are huts in the North of Europe

he has heard of some in Taprobana

it was said it was raining when Adam left

but was there rain before the flood?

but if there was fruit from the branch it must have rained

there are umbrellas on *Le Pont de l'Europe*

where this writer toys with the beginnings of a shower

having a roof over our heads

and hats also

apparently swallows, rooks, bees and storks
were the first builders

they exchanged the cone for the cube
putting a tent on top for a roof

now seven of the world's largest cities are in Asia

we will be staying in the Pyongyang Ryugyong Hotel

there is always a need for an agreeable location to hold a party

drunkenly clinging to each other

in those country temples dedicated to love

the streets hereabouts filled with waifs and strays

eating *pommes frites* out of paper cones

shelter from severities with reed and cane

searching the bloat ring of road stores

to build their dwellings

the size of ocean going liners

journeying to the furthest countries to bring forth bounty

I will marry an islander with long growing Tahiti hair

such is the origin of the navy

and civil planning

at the end of the 15th century Moscow had not one house built of stone

only huts of wood moss and logs

the long gallop of horses across the steppe

In Monomotapa all the dwellings are of wood

fish are born to swim (in ornamental Zen pools)

and birds to song

those lacking a certain kind of intelligence (liking the gas-fired barbecue)

build their lives out of skin and bone

of quadrupeds and marine monsters

rows of Jonah Homes with sea-bone features *bella natura*

if Palladio had lived before the flood

the city below the sea

those of the Icelanders are built of small pieces of stone bound with slurry

the name of the inventor of perfume is not known
(Mr Pee Pong did table tennis)
        although attar of roses had been discovered
        walking through gum trees (see above)

and
cedar at night
        the warmth
and aroma of resin overcame
me as did
        the iris in Illyria
        the nard in Gaul
        and the pomegranate at Attica

reminded me of her pink flesh
her rings upon my fingers
my fingers in her toes

Shepherds   spent their summers inside
the leafy shelter of trees
(often with the odd goat herder)

it is a pleasant sight when viewed from a distance

they enjoy the fresh taste of barbecued lamb
with a fresh mountain herb rocket salad and a grained mustard
        dressing

some black olives
some black bread

the banyan tree grows near River Acesius
the leaves look like birds' wings
big ones

the fruit contains a sweet juice

the President of our country sits there sometimes with his dog
he has a dog
the dog has fleas

this tree is a plantain

Alexander gave orders that no one should touch this fruit

therefore for sweetening they relied on honey
this is spring honey whose comb is made of pollen

honey comes out of the air as rising stars
when Sirius shines over Mt Ida

SOME QUESTIONS CONCERNING CIVILIZATION

the King   lived here or a little further
accessible by public bus
under the trees in the town square popular with the young
large ships no longer stopping here
the city rises in steep tiers
the bus leaving every five minutes 4Km east of the city
takes you eight miles south until you come to the point
from the wharves where the ferries dock
to cross the river   the distance is less than a mile
and can be covered by foot or on donkey

as soon as you enter the West Court (the ancient
ceremonial entrance) the sky and the earth
are still

sirens dart across the stairway
a painted vulture death black

the King sitting in the cool shade

if you enter by the North Gate you will view the lustral bath
a place for purification and the King's quick dip
most probably the oldest in Europe

the docking station is at the Southern end
it does a brisk business
if its drugs, women, men or boys you want

you will need every second for sight seeing
you should leave one half hour before the 6:00 a.m. crossing

the road festooned
the common held theory that the track was the way to a Royal
    summer villa
the young King's house
in the evening when the trappers have gone you can read the
cuneiform correspondence between Egypt and Syria
a Post Office and all you can drink
rent a bike
he who lives in the sky
he who looks down upon
a volume of despair

the trees festooned
and in the evening they serve local wine from the wood,
the pin point light between the mountains and the trees
catching the sparkle on the church at the western end of the
    main street
as we drive towards the public gardens

an outburst of joy overcame me

time passing like rain falling momentarily

the waterfront is lined with mansions
as far away as America
to sell grain to France
a road leads back down in a great circle
there are 365 churches
bringing women in by the boat load
the finest chandeliers and stucco saw wealth accrue
to service the men butchering one another like animals
great one-eyed hawks, vultures
putting up drones over the city
a scattering of holiday villas
on the other side there is good swimming to have from the rocks
another circle and another
from the King with one eye
to the men with none at all
tickets can be bought from the departure quay
and the sky streaming with it
and the summer flowers
pick me ups as the world forever formelts and burns

The View from Space (Sub-Orbital)

Malevich envisaged a floating city
'on the path of the absence of weight humanity walks'
one inhabitant was Yuri
Malevich was 34 in 1920 writes *sputniks*
looking down from above is the future

from coast to coast
Chinese consumer goods are held in reserve
sweat shop blouses
'A roll of silk from K'ang-fu, width 2 feet 2 inches,
length 40 feet, weight 25 ounces, value 618 pieces of money'

how much will she cost
the other woman could be a madam
The Procuress 1656

Themes for Developing a Treaty

Japenese pirates were called *waegu*
the brigands from the country of Wa
or as *wako*   in the plum tree coloured river Kum

Chong Chi used cannon fire to scatter Japanese ships
1500 wako were relieved of their heads
little was spoken by the wako for many years to come

wako became a name used by brigands
a mixed bag of blood   Chinese renegades
Portuguese freebooters and Japanese mercenaries

the Chinese pirate Wang Zhi was caught and beheaded in 1551

THE AGE OF WARRING

Sengoku Jidai (The Age of Battles or Warring States)

light feet were foot soldiers

an opportunity to gain land and power

to settle disputes

there is always betrayal and defection

when the wars end the Imperial capital
becomes nothing but a stage

our Emperor a puppet
for the use of the Tokugawa shogun

DIRK BROCADE

women carried dirks in waist sashes

in brocade

the *nagunata* was their weapon

roaming castles at night

the red, black and white currant flowering bush
imprinted on their wear

a *rônin* was a wave person
a sword for hire

they took the tonsure

the basis of the economy was rice

a unit of rice was a *koku*

one *koku* is 120 litres

    a series of connected thoughts
    whereby the poet, usually a disappointing individual,
    thinks and puts his / her thinks down on paper

    down on paper

Heidegger

Was Heidegger a Buddhist

did he copulate in the woods *(Holzwege)*
with a maiden of the woods
(do you remember her subsequent children and the accompanying
    illustration)

there to contemplate being and perhaps a mushroom or two

do you remember the Woods

can I be a Buddhist

I'd call you (you need mountains to yodel) my nymph of the woods

did Heidegger suffer from nympholepsy
or was he too concerned with hammers and nails
and wood for his wooden hut

did he have rat poison

I must get back to you

I must return by the ship of the mind

Chemins qui mènent nulle part
leading me on letting me go

if I yodel across mountain thyme
would you answer
(those tracks which wind purposely from one point to another)
the odd goat and goat herder looking on

the odd whistle from the wolf
Mrs Woods calling the sheep in

we could retrace our steps through the woods which lead nowhere

I could cook for you (wild mushrooms)

you could introduce your children and your husband the
    woodcutter

are there trees in the Himalayan foothills

Chaise Longue

In the mind room of the brain there's a chaise longue
where the world can be switched off /

>what wood would that be?
>what did Poussin get off on?

the wise man might be in such a room—if wise men there are
(I know some wise guys but that's not the same
I know some wise women *in situ*)

Did he paint standing up?

Poets lay on beds reading books by other poets—usually friends

Southey and Coleridge tried to solve the mind body situation by
>taking
a lot of illegal substances—narcosis by drip feed—pollen clouds
making Coleridge sneeze like a bee storm and rise from the
>chaise longue
dreaming of the life to come

Eurydice looks distressed in Poussin's painting
(is she being chaste?)
Orpheus fails to see her

In the mind room many things are lost—this is efferent.
Just as Mont St-Victoire is situated beyond the railway cut
the eye too travels
through a group of wedding guests

>	Did salon artists recline on a chaise longue
>	so that the mind is perhaps not *in situ*—at least memory
>	has been carried off (untraced)

to be taken away is sometimes pleasurable (perhaps into
      disambiguation)
Southey and Coleridge wanted to go to America in 1794
"each man to take a mild and lovely woman for his wife"
(an overdose of opiate perfusion, no doubt)

Cézanne took Poussin apart
painting directly onto the canvas

In the mind room many things are taken for granted (second
order neural patterning)

we know where the cork screw is
the strangler's cord
and the well used wrench which removes the heart
the sleep forum packed with chaise longue

waking up and coming back to life (re-entry)

Eurydice only seen by a fisherman (is this a reverse of Orpheus'
      earlier failure)

a pull cord light bulb—click

THE GREENHOUSE EFFECT

Remove the cumbersome cucumber
Who knows its genus
What a difference an *i* could make

The first farmers strove across nature before settling
I become settled after nature
(Though it is difficult to know what my nature is)
I am prone to relapse
(Remedy: crushed cucumber seeds in rainwater)

For days you could wander
I am told
And never meet a fellow traveller
(I have ditched the cucumber)
Nature is the source of all axioms
And we the source of all her troubles

Here is Mr Potato Man—the obesity effect!
Men dropping from trees
Like wartime parachutists
Into the fields like seeds where
Now doppelganger housing estates appear
Boosting the homogenous economic spread

Do androids dream of eccentric sheep

The dildo

When I lie on my bed *à la* Ted Berrigan reading the French
    immortals what
Three thoughts do I have in my head
(I feel I need a footnote here)

(Back to the cucumber)
(I feel I need another footnote here)
It contains multiples

Absinthe with opium
Lenny Bruce
And a number of troubadours

Che Guevara's Cigar

We go to Argentina in the cinema

What do I know of the world—comes from
picture books and night lights
pictures of gauchos
pineapples
oil rigs
sombrero sunshine

you me and physical geography

Nine Queens is a set of stamps (everything's a con)

Olson writing $1,000,000 for example of
$3,000,000
paid to Castro in 1960 was it—1961
    WAS DIRECTLY FROM THE MOB, BOSTON
raised over the phone overnight by—for Robt
        Kennedy—by Cardinal Cushing

also backing both sides pre revolution

Lucky Luciano released from prison takes over Sicily for the MOB
    and USA end of WWII

also travels to Cuba

Fidel still alive today (the exploding cigar—poisoned pen—the
    man stabbed with an umbrella)

Personally authorised by US attorney general Robert Kennedy

King Herod wheeling and dealing

An actor riding a motorcycle from his parents house to a girl I
    loved in the cinema

What else will he appear in (disguise)

The grass waving in the films of Terrence Malick as in *The Song
    of Solomon*

Casino

Tonight (so direct & warm—it's July)

pissing against the wind

and life like a tortoise goes fleetingly by in the early morning rain

at least the weather balloon is up

would you like some tortoise meat

some turtle soup

Life is at least complicated

and then we sigh

and turn over

too many times without regret

typed on the thinnest of papers

The Good Shepherd

The poem is particularly obscure
      we read of a Caucasian man
           with a Negro woman

The resolution breaks down

Is it a translation from the Russian

One of the lines to focus on is
the mosquito netting

Mosquito netting can be found predominantly in Africa
Southeast Asia
Tropical climates

For the *greater good* says Robert Redford in *The Spy Game*

Brad Pitt, young and in love

Here Matt Damon decoding her moves / motives of Clover,
      Angelina Jolie

In moments of myth
I will drink fragrant coconut juice
a little alcohol through a pink recycled straw
relief from pain says Lucretius★

The window curtains (why window?) have
a distinctive pattern on them
of baobab trees
also seen in Africa

Next to the curtains
the building's balustrade
There's a pigeon
(always a pigeon with another one)
mostly found in urban areas
town squares
(rain slashed, abandoned and reflective)
when men wore hats and Che a beret

Reading between the lines there's an aeroplane
It's a jet
Taking off
1000 feet above the ground
which further suggests a large urban area
when you clear everything away
there's always the lover's voice
a distinct ring-back tone

Clover's conversation echoes the poem I'm trying to decode
Siren
Hiss on the line
Cuneiform breakage
almost indistinct
fades

Linguists tell me her accent is French
She's kissed the one kiss that has stopped his heart

There's her whispered word I can't make out
There's an unidentifiable noise washing out her love whispers
An air-raid?

Cochinos is Spanish for *pigs*

Is there something here

How long (ever) to a definition as to exactly where we are?

★Do you not see that nature is clamouring for two things only, a body free from pain, a mind released from worry

Anthropology

Up in the mountains
the Cave-Dwellers hoard cinnamon sticks
in order to add flavour to Pygmy Stew
EVEN DWARFS STARTED SMALL
anything that breathes shouldn't be eaten
I'm beginning to wonder about Natural History
The President's dog has fleas (did I mean Pygmy Shrew)
The President has a Pygmy Shrew
Did Alexander Pope have a sex life
Noddy had Big Ears

Natural Material

Until the time of Egypt's pyramid builders
the Sahara was not the hyper arid wasteland of today
but a land of lakes, cress and water-lily

For the first farmers
Mr and Mrs Bong Tong and their offshoots
it was the bottle-gourd which held pride of place

It can be found as far apart as Thailand and Mexico

The gourd makes an excellent container
they are light, durable and free of charge

Like the gourd the coconut will float
its fruit will stay viable in salt water
for three months or more

to store eggs in
to stand on top of the microwave
the ornate egg-timer filled with ancient sand from Egypt

The Making of Mong

the Indian Princess rides a white horse

it's not a bronco

and carries the eye (assorted sequins—full and half moons)

accompanied by Mong the Merciful

these two lovers ride the Punjab hills

is this their happiness

the night sky flashing twin set pearls

a sign can be a revelation

later they will make Mong Kung of all the world

The genesis of poetry. The *Making of Mong* came about through insomnia and a misreading of John Updike's *Just Looking, Essays on Art*. Without my glasses I read his *Moving Along* as Making Mong—the picture in question being *Riding By Moonlight,* circa 1780, Pahari miniature in Kangra style.

The Citadel of Love

Krishna carried out his love making with the gopris

a woman blames her cat for scratches inflicted by her lover

is happiness a mood

is her happiness a mood

Heidegger writes that he is always in a mood

another wears a peacock shirt

can charm the snakes out of the trees

they usually do a two by two

the sun setting over the Punjab hills

almost a wet blob of sealing wax (Hungarian paprika)

also the moon-apple white with a bite taken from it

Moon Rush (for Yuri Gargarin)

Wally found himself ageing with his readers
His poetry had become tinder dry, his prose a withering briar

Old Doc Holliday was at that time
Before he became a convinced sociopath
a Shepherd living in a two-wheeled donkey cart
of an evening he'd play cards with Wally

All they had in the world, besides each other,
were a kerosene cook stove
sleeping bags and a washing pale

Sometimes at night they bred
heavenly stars in cosmological liquids

Wally's grandfather led a mule train in Baker, Oregon

Some said first settler Indian blood ran through his veins

When one night
Wally's boot scrapped out the embers of the fire
and he threw down steaming coffee grains
he foreknew the signs amongst the ashes

Doc would go on to meet William Bonney

At first Wally's writing was a hit. Sales were good. Pickings
         were rich.

Doc, a fledgling peacekeeper, abandoned the law, moving
to Van Nuys, California

to become a full-time body builder and woodsman in porn
    movies
and fan of the *Mothers of Invention*

After Wally passed away the demand for his work intensified

Especially selected by NASA
the first astronauts back from the moon read his work

A Bright New Thing Has Dawned

Wally experienced vicissitudes
as he walked from Steubenville, Ohio
to the state's southern villages

days then always dawned with bright new mornings
against dazzling prehistoric backdrops

his was a delicate touch
ephemeral dust motes caught
by his pen

he'd write across ice to deliver fire

Military training at the academy
taught him how to use a gun
and be a tracker
he wrote about wolves in the wilderness
and hostile landscapes devoid of man's menace

later road engineering brought new highways

progress taking them to the moon

despite his early work on Dante, Virgil and Horace
he frequently felt the sting of rejection

heartbroken he cried into his mother's arms

she begged him to stop masturbating

Three Hudson River School Poems

Catskill on a fast steamboat
later a train to Tarrytown
checking into a hostelry at the top of the fall

the sun orange and gold on leaf
nun's white through a dark chasm
from a cave this side of the far waters

filled with tiny tourists
well educated, gesticulating from their frozen hearts

what combination of talent, wealth,
opportunity and time
brought them to this place

to view a land in summer
a reminder of constant change
in tumbles between rocks and trees

Viagra from Goat Island

dreams of word pictures come to mind
speaking Hindi in English

nuanced light adumbrating the gentle shape

the upper and lower registers of water and sky

vanilla

I felt my legs tremble

'This' gurgled one happy one
'is X with the root left out'

for 25¢ doggers could stare
sometimes using binoculars

transfixed

'Behold!' a marvel of the Western World
is before you

COINCIDENCE

Yosemite Valley from Glacier Point
more open space tourists skimpily
dressed through mist blobs
holding the commanding position
about the size of a landscape
inclement weather causing goose bumps

an instrumentality of light (a torch)
offers up detail
just this side of fuzziness

miles away Wally stretches his arms from
canyon to canyon
to the horizon and limitlessly
self love to either side

as in the novels of Karl May
a confidence man
Old Shatterhand in *Der Schatz im Silbersee*

and *Washington Crossing the Delaware*

FRANS VAN MERIS: THE SOLDIER AND THE PROSTITUTE

motifs like rivers run through
1611 Gabriel Rollenhagen's *Book of Emblems*
the use of the window for procurement and seduction
causing the natural essence to surge

foolish love I feel like a lemon
a third party
Perch' io stesso mi strusi

the clients only moderately pissed, moderately vulgar

it's the picture of an idea of society
husbands, marriage, clothes, wealth, comfort, vice

the rug from an original city

river valley market

an exchange economy

Mount Ida Zeus

He wanted her but she was married

She made arrangements, assignations
seeing him at night

Briefly, quickly he mobbed her gently (text defective)

it was dark as hell
said Constantinos at Aptera

one room for Demeter and one for Persephone

of course they used iron to make bullets★

and bubble gum★★ to hold up the toilet seat

she was a beauty that he kept hidden

for years my secret

★Hesiod attributes the forging of iron to Crete, to the Dactyl of Mt Ida
★★bubble gum was my solution

African Inquisition

the hammer dots his head
dink donk

the exact cranial spot
fractures

his teeth fall out like hail
(but only a handful, short lived)
moth balls on asphalt

I'm left gnawing for breath
he could vomit a live octopus

as so and always in contrast

peaceful snowfalls cover the hills
bending river valley

blood also over the plasma screen

Sierra Leone

a few stoned bandits playing cards

a taste for slaughter

Freetown, he said
let me interrogate him
before you eat him

cheap flights available

Contradictions

demons threaten the sick man in the third register
the plot is advanced by dreams which presage future events

dreams come in threes
winds in sevens

women de-seed men to read their minds
the child she is to bear will become king

L'HOMME DU TRAIN

having for single luggage a bag of voyage
and all that's in it

the former teacher dreamed himself adventurous
all seemed opposed him, the barber, the baker's woman

too much of all the same

thinking of things to change his life
who will sympathize in a small town of small minds
to leave his wife behind—his house and roof

reading in his book and quoting by heart poetry

TRANSPORT

Norbert and Martial riding their mobillettes
one of a number of recalled impressions
others occur in Belgium

Now it's 1967 *Mouchette*

she making the best apple pie, sugaring the apple
slices, they sweat

as now, nobody to see it with or talk to about you

L'enfant, burying things, hiding,
retrieving, and of course Rosetta's ethical complications
a memory like memory
like consciousness

where is that
or
Dick who never read a poem in his life
but rode a Lambretta circa 1967
and I'm on the Grand Boulevards
and think *How do they impress me?*
troubling me

The Queen of Puddings

she will not

She will not return
I being dead to the heart
This is the slippery slope of Switzerland
She returns my post
The heart burns through my synthetic knit-wear

Night life has disappeared, daylight too
I climb a north face to vomit into Austria
This poem pierced by her eyes
They are my stars above the earth's mantle

She can never return as that girl I longed for
Now in my clumsiness
I have to gut the fish and peel the pears
They were so small in your hands

I bet there's a huge pear tree somewhere
Over-ripe with wanting

Off the coast there's a useless homemade raft

Now all the belongings I have are worthless

the sentence

The sentence you gave me was unfair
From which I never recovered

You were proportionate
Fine skin, smooth bone and soft lips
Now I am all head

I would rather there were
Poisonous insects in the air
Instead of my howling in the rain
But it is October when there were
Different colours in your eyes

I am restless, so much so,
I will never recover. It's far too late.
Now I have a stick and toupee.
Poetry is useless in these situations
As it is to most others

I look

I look at you
I am all to sea
A small oar less boat
Noah's potato eyes

I refuse metaphor
To analogise
Vaseline won't help
or vile health food extracts

It's your birthday
And I'd kiss you
Later I will destroy
This poem

I don't want to be here
The sea is wet
But it can be beautiful
And the sky too is optimal

Leading

Leading a level sort of life
(Although delusion may be part of it)
I have sorted my bottom drawer
Order to be maintained

Ah but it was always May and but briefly
You a fine and rare extract,
Some exciting travail to China

Just once you were
A place of rockeries, grottoes
and winding hill garden pathways

Now there are new plateau lines
Sun splattered mud
and the gentlest of sea breezes

Is this what love and anger come to
A horizon line

Waiting for a boat to fish up a bomb

Nineteen

Your face must be nineteen
But there was no painter
A chain of lakes I can't swim through
And nowhere to recover

Are the bridges lifted or sunk
Crossing the divide
Why dig these holds
If there is nothing to rest on

I have a bad heart
It was best when breathless
Strangely when everything meant nothing
Putting highlights in your hair

How can all this be safe
And oddly only in one place

The darkly lacquered handled brush
The air-filled scented summer room

consumer choice

Men go bald
And fences blow over
Like a koan
Who says false teeth chatter

There is mud on the land
Where seabirds rifle beaks for grub
Geese dive into pâté tins
On deserted health farms

We are food-chained to this
Bemoaning a riddle
Of the supermarket state

Clouds of skate
Freefall through
The North Atlantic Drift
Of the deepfreeze

Fat well-fed Buddhas cling
to uncertifiable warranties
Coconut oil scent from tanning booths

The way is of course
To forget the shelf

we should never

We should never have become involved
Not that involution lifted me
A submarine to surface

You as white cherry-blossom bloomed
My speech centres failed
I thought of you as
A foreign language

In a catchment area I
Filled with common cold

Nothing moved
At the bottom of the lake
My arms tied and the air
Choked in my chest

Later the abyssal wind howled
Like an out of tune radio

A series of arguments and medication

what a day

God what a horrible day—
Week, month, year.
The wind howls and I'm
Sunk in your chair

A line of coke makes me numb
My friends have left me
(They couldn't have been my friends)
There are thieves on the street

From the valley of the road
Between two thimbles
The sky is lead in the river
There are no letters

I will live my remaining years
Lost in thought
Yodelling in Switzerland
Stacking the freezer with monkfish

what now

What now
To take up deep-sea diving
Flustered at what we did

Your young girl hands
Or trek to be
Thrashed with birch in Finland

Discovering the sting of rays
and the bind of seaweed

Body-trapped with no air
Who cared
Riding the vertiginous slopes

Now abyssal regrets
Melting in the snow
Skiing away from me

I wondered

I wondered what a switch-blade was
Until you left
The birds flew like rocks
Winter clogged the arteries

Ted said Joe had a shrew of a wife
Why stick with her
The moon collapsed like a condom
Torrents swept the sky

Joe hung his head like a dead crane
I never believed a single word
(neither unbelieved one either)

Everything stopped then

I can still feel the trembling in your legs

And the words I make up
make repetitions of your body

Joe felt the blade of her mouth

I will quit to take up wrestling
With an iron or cleaning
(Something domestic). It indicates survival
The unswatted fly on the pane.

more

Less of the subject
But more, more of you
Ice-cream whipped forays
The clouds you recline on

Why fulfil myself with such thoughts
Such foreign lines
It reminds of buffoon parlour etiquette

Of rhyming couples

Stiff with lacquer and glossed
With health and beauty
I grovel at your plate
Longing to lick it

Slinking off like the guilty dog
To my eternal retreat

Taking up Buddhism
Practicing my dharanis
Arranging dahlias

Discomforting sounds of nature
Disturb me, birds in twos, butterflies
The ice-house drip
Of Chinese water torture

gulf

You are cold in your hotel
It is in the far North
Somewhere near Trondheim

The articulate circle of
Your lips—a sheen of ice gloss
That only your smile can light

I'm lost here
Building a small toboggan
Which the authorities
will disavow

Your husky voice
Thrills me
Trailing motifs (voice prints)

How annoying it is
Not to be a hot air thermal being
able to engulf you in abeyance

white rush

Insignia you are behind me

A rusted tomato sun
Somewhere in Spain
When bitter oranges ripen

All I can see of the past
are the nets open for harvest

Undressed in the warm wind to
The finger-tips of your olive skin

I always wished to swim like a turtle
Or fly like a dolphin
Hung up in liquid
Being alive through your hot mouth

When the snow finally
falls and melts
I will jump from the lintel into
The white rush of air

My hands unable to grasp you

the queen of puddings

Iceland seems so cold
No she said
Making a fool of myself

How many fools is that?

And look how the dish turned out

The Queen of Puddings

I could say the mountains
Are topped with meringue

That I have fallen in love

I have corrected the imbalance
Keeping abreast of it all

But my anxieties slide

I toboggan vertiginously down

I dream of iced metaphors

melts

What is a rope dancer?
What is a lap dancer?
I'm so naive you take advantage of me
That's why I'm into ski-wear

The wolves of Lapland won't chase me off
From milking reindeer or
wanting to fish with a pole
Through a hole in the ice

We will eat it sushi accompanied by
The clean taste of Finnish vodka
A spit of lime zest on your tongue

I intend to collapse like
An overcooked cabbage when
My time bomb goes off
Pssssssssh. That is not steam from the sauna
But sweat from my brow
I'm a hot thermal spring

Ice thawing and footprints fading
I'm being reminded now to
adopt a more measured pace to life
Filling myself with the pain I'll never forget

sky-diver

Snow all day.
I've frozen out your cacophony
Of signs—my handful of your
Scattered charms. What did you
Take me for? Sucking on a
Love heart makes no redress.

It was nothing—knowing now
You are in Venice researching Giotto
Hair to your middle back
Dancing with your partner
Moving your lip-scented stencilled smile
Over his body

Here everyday life is stifling
That is what my advance has brought
The odd charitable penny for drought
Or the ever ongoing disasters of war.

All I'm left with is leisure
Walking in heavy boots
Across an ocean floor.

There are patterns and tracks in the snow
Of fallen sky-divers
Eidolons only of coincidence
Those who have melted away in your arms

I will make a snowman of sorts
And surround it with cereal figures
This will be my grotto

nip and tuck

Can I drown in snow?
Flying into space covered in down
Cocooned softly?

Does your name retain meaning?

Do they hunt eider?
Do they eat your flesh?
White chocolate coated
Mother of pearl passion fruit!

Butterflies never crash
Swapping body parts

Are they engulfed by bats?

Under the coverlet
You are now my ghost
A thin wisp to wish with

Can a fish drown?

Pulled back as I am
Through water

shades

Green words are mountains—bumps
On the horizon
What shade of mood are you?

My immune system shredded

Are those rocks I see reflected in your eyes?
My glasses bring you closer

They are in fact memories

Shrines built on summits in the Zen clear air

What words are you?

Do they change and interchange?

Above the tree line there are more bumps

Is that phrenology?

On the threshold
I wave the odds and go for it

But you're a long way off exhausted
By my rapture

That's physical geography

Rising to the top
knowing where to get off
knowing what to get off on

health care

In my dream
You were fat and bald
The terror to come!

But in my real dream
You were as you were.

The doctor told me to forget you
distract myself

If only there was a photograph
Other than the immaterial one

I noticed too that the doctor
Was bald and fat
That's a fact and not a dream

I've lost faith in dreams

My aim the
Perfect body
And the useless mind

tantalize

Today the air is as crisp as filo-blue
What is it worth? You
Tantalize me with your words

But you've gone
And my moments past

A few snowdrops
A sound or two from early birds

We argued (again)

Coat huddled winter
I waited for you
Climbing the funicular

Now I wait for the year to turn
For the fuck to work

I wait and wait
But that was long, long ago

I leaf the morning news

It does not change
It recycles down the same path
And toots *fuck you* at the dead

dance lessons

You lay with the King of France
Dancing the Fandango (if I've spelt it correctly)
Sequin fronted blouse

Vomiting into the sink

I shot at fish in remorse
To make them lame
Not always rational I would have him guillotined
Washing off the sticky herring scales

Wanting to be gobbled up

I'm obviously strung out

Waiting to learn that tune on the piano
Walk along the keys without leaving a trace

volvic

What's so good about Olive
She's had her womb cleaned out
Popeye's had the snip
Life moves on

My understanding grows
I can spell Volvo
But there's little I understand of Sweden

At least I can say *Hello* to strangers
Sometimes I've thought
Of making a contribution—VSO

Why didn't I choose a career
Instead of making jokes out of Pan yang
Or at least backpack to Phnom Pen

Never moving out of the same street
Reading the same newspaper
Shagging the girl next door

plain facts

Rosie screams and pounds the dog
No matter
In the picture she pulls at her hair
feeds it crisps

At the wedding
She's running with a hoop
Bombs bang the building

At the funeral
They shoot the mourners

They arrest the uncle
(Something to do with meat)

Potato peelings with water make soup

A dog pisses in fear

I'm full of resentment and anger

Rosie's changed her mind

My pocket full of scratchings for the dog

something to look forward to

In the film hearts have tumbled

I'm thinking of garrotting
Of not waking up
To porridge
And washing the pan

My heart is faint
Wanting Parque Guell
To be full of poets I can talk to
Instead of dogs, whores and thieves

What is the point

This blank as snow piece of paper
Will become a map
Perhaps a duck pond

A track or trail to a precipice
Site specific
And abseil from the top
Inviting further (poetic) speculation

wishful thinking

You are beautiful and I am trapped
A single seater only
Your essence beyond me

My thoughts are bound by practicalities

Take off and petrol fumes

(Donkeys figure in my dreams
Always in the bottom right hand corner
Airy creatures, bird sirens, bats

For lunch it would be something simple and French
For dinner the opera
A moth
A gnat, at a pinch)

Most probably all will be spectacular
Rising stars, comets and creamy moonlets

(This is where illness begins and ends)

The plane's flashing lights are jetting away
The submarine's sinking out to sea
Just as intended

It's the meditative life from now on
(Audrey Hepburn as a nun)

Idling time with poetry
Making a better place of the world on paper

future plans

A gap in living
One who died on Tuesday
Planning a world cruise

I forfeit all

I planned on you

You'll have wrinkles now
A dog
Grown up children
And Latvian oil interests

I'm entering a new phase
About to study religion (in theory)
A side order to life
As I am in an Autumn or Cheyenne
Of confusion

Driving down the Pacific rim
Rude thoughts of us
Fill me once more with vigour

my blood ran

You dropped from my sight (memory)
Some winter thaw
As cold as Austrian Alps
Rescued you (my St Bernadette)

My blood ran again
No longer stiff like unwarmed syrup

I reread your words once more
Precisely on a card
Indian dancers

You were always the source of my dilemma
Flowing west to east

It's too late now
Hemmed in

But the Austrian mountains
Still echo alpine flowers

The scent of the secrets only we knew

www.ingramcontent.com/pod-product-compliance
Lightning Source LLC
Chambersburg PA
CBHW031156160426
43193CB00008B/386